I0017150

AI: The Furture Was Yesterday

by

Al Abbott D' Monet

Copyright © 2023 Al Abbott D'Monet.
All rights reserved. Including the right to reproduce this book or portions thereof, in any form. No part of this text may be reproduced in any form without the express written permission of the author.

ISBN: 9798393111366

Contents

Introduction

The future was yesterday!

Artificial intelligence is progressing at a breakneck pace, far faster than anyone anticipated. Self-driving cars populate the roads. AI systems detect diseases, generate stunning new molecules, and outperform humans at complex strategy games. Robots are collaborating with people in factories and homes, learning from every interaction.

Each day brings a new breakthrough, a new record shattered, a new height of machine intelligence scaled. The pace of progress leaves us little time to grapple with its implications. By the time we absorb one technological miracle, a dozen more have appeared. The future is happening all around us, whether we realize it or not. All that was once considered science fiction is now within our grasp—and AI's potential is only starting to unfold.

The machines are not just on the rise—they are on the run. The future that once seemed so distant is upon us, and yesterday's dreams of advanced AI are today's reality. The age of intelligent machines has dawned, not with a whimper but with a bang. This is the story of artificial intelligence's breakneck advance, told by tracing its restless race into the future that caught up to the present far sooner than we ever thought possible. The future, it seems, arrived yesterday. We just have some catching up to do.

AI: The Furture Was Yesterday

Chapter 1: An Introduction into AI

What is AI?

Artificial intelligence (AI) is the scientific and engineering effort aimed at creating intelligent machines that can learn, reason, and carry out tasks like humans. AI draws on knowledge from fields such as computer science, mathematics, psychology, linguistics, and philosophy to power machines with human-like cognition.

AI does not simply strive to copy human thinking. Rather, its goal is to develop systems that can learn, adapt, make data-driven decisions, and accomplish complex goals beyond human ability alone.

Some of the hallmarks of human-level intelligence that AI systems aim to replicate include:

•Visual perception: The ability to identify and process information from images, photos, and videos in the way

humans do. This enables AI systems to classify objects, scenes, faces, etc.

•Speech recognition: Converting the sounds of human speech into text. This allows people to interact with AI systems through voice interfaces.

•Natural language processing: Analyzing human language as a way to understand semantics, nuance meaning, generate responses, and convert between languages.

•Decision making: Using knowledge, logic, and probabilistic reasoning to evaluate options, make judgments, and choose a course of action, especially in uncertain conditions.

•Problem solving: Figuring out ways to achieve a goal or objective that may require multiple steps or non-obvious solutions. This involves skills such as planning, learning from experience, and adapting approach to obstacles.

There are several different types of AI, each with its own strengths and weaknesses. The most common types of AI are:

•Reactive AI: Reactive AI is the most basic type of AI and is focused solely on reacting to current events in the environment. It does not have any memory of past events or the ability to predict future events. Examples of reactive AI include chess-playing computers and facial recognition software.

•Limited Memory AI: Limited Memory AI is able to learn from past experiences and use that knowledge to make decisions in the future. However, it is still limited in its ability to predict future events. Examples of limited memory AI include self-driving cars and personal assistants like Siri and Alexa.

•Theory of Mind AI: Theory of Mind AI is able to understand the mental states of others and use that understanding to make decisions. This type of AI is still in the early stages of development and is not yet widely used.

•Self-Aware AI: Self-aware AI is a hypothetical type of AI that is able to understand its own existence and consciousness. It is still purely a theoretical concept and has not yet been achieved.

AI is used in a wide range of applications, from speech recognition and language translation to medical diagnosis and financial forecasting. Some of the most common applications of AI include:

•Natural Language Processing (NLP) Natural language processing (NLP) is a branch of AI that focuses on enabling computers to understand and interpret human language. NLP involves breaking down human language into its component parts, such as words and sentences, and then analyzing those parts to extract meaning. NLP is used in applications such as voice assistants, chatbots, and language translation software.

•Machine Learning: Machine learning is a field of

computer science that involves developing algorithms and models that enable computers to learn and improve from experience without being explicitly programmed.

This is achieved by feeding large amounts of data into the machine learning model and using statistical techniques to identify patterns and make predictions. Machine learning has revolutionized many industries, including healthcare, finance, and transportation, by enabling the creation of intelligent systems that can automate complex tasks and make accurate predictions. From image and speech recognition to recommendation systems and fraud detection, machine learning has become an essential tool for solving many real-world problems.

•Robotics: Robotics is a field that combines AI with mechanical engineering to create intelligent machines that can perform physical tasks. Robotics involves designing and building machines that can sense their environment, make decisions based on that environment, and then take actions to accomplish tasks. Robots are used in a wide range of industries, from manufacturing and logistics to healthcare and education.

•Computer Vision: Computer vision is a branch of AI that focuses on enabling computers to interpret and analyze visual data. Computer vision involves using algorithms to analyze images and video, and then extract meaningful information from that data. Computer vision is used in applications such as facial recognition, object recognition, and self-driving cars.

AI can be divided into two broad categories: symbolic AI and machine learning. Symbolic AI involves the use of rules and logic to make decisions, while machine learning involves training machines to learn from data.

Symbolic AI is based on the idea that intelligence can be reduced to a set of rules and logic. This approach involves creating a knowledge base of facts and rules, and then using logical inference to make decisions based on that knowledge. Symbolic AI is still used in some applications, such as expert systems and rule-based decision-making, but it has largely been superseded by machine learning.

Machine learning, on the other hand, involves training machines to learn from data. This approach is based on the idea that intelligence can be learned through experience, just like humans do. Machine learning involves feeding large amounts of data into an algorithm, which then learns to recognize patterns and make predictions based on that data.

There are several different types of machine learning, including supervised learning, unsupervised learning, and reinforcement learning. Supervised learning involves training an algorithm on a labeled dataset, where each data point is labeled with the correct answer. The algorithm then learns to recognize patterns in the data and make predictions based on those patterns.

Supervised learning is used in applications such as image recognition and natural language processing.

Unsupervised learning, on the other hand, involves training an algorithm on an unlabeled dataset, where there are no correct answers. The algorithm then learns to recognize patterns in the data and group similar data points together. Unsupervised learning is used in applications such as clustering and anomaly detection.

Reinforcement learning involves training an algorithm to make decisions based on rewards and punishments. The algorithm is given a goal to achieve, and then learns to take actions that maximize the reward and minimize the punishment. Reinforcement learning is used in applications such as game playing and robotics.

In order for AI to be effective, it must be based on high-quality data. This data must be clean, accurate, and relevant to the problem at hand. However, collecting and managing large amounts of data can be a daunting task. This has led to the rise of big data technologies, which are designed to enable the processing and analysis of large amounts of data.

One of the key technologies in the big data space is Hadoop, an open-source software framework that enables the distributed processing of large datasets across clusters of computers. Hadoop is widely used in the industry for tasks such as data warehousing, data processing, and data analysis.

Another key technology in the big data space is Apache Spark, an open-source data processing engine that is designed for speed and ease of use. Spark is used for a wide range of tasks, including data processing, machine learning, and real-time streaming.

AI also relies heavily on cloud computing, which enables access to powerful computing resources on demand. Cloud computing provides a scalable and flexible infrastructure for AI applications, allowing organizations to easily scale up or down as needed.

The major cloud providers, such as Amazon Web Services, Microsoft Azure, and Google Cloud Platform, all offer AI services and tools that can be used to build and deploy AI applications. In order for AI to be successful, it must be based on ethical principles and values. This includes ensuring that AI is transparent, explainable, and unbiased. It also means ensuring that AI is developed and deployed in a way that respects human rights and values.

To this end, several organizations have developed principles and guidelines for ethical AI. For example, the European Union has developed a set of guidelines for trustworthy AI, which includes principles such as transparency, accountability, and fairness. The IEEE has also developed a set of ethical guidelines for AI, which includes principles such as transparency, accountability, and privacy.

In sum, artificial intelligence is advancing rapidly and promises to enrich our lives in profound and manifold ways. From conversational AI to robotics, intelligent systems are shaping how we communicate, work, learn, access information, and more.

Yet as AI grows more capable and integrated into our day-to-day lives, it also introduces vital questions that demand diligent stewardship. How can we maximize the benefits of AI while minimizing unavoidable harms?

How do we guarantee AI progresses as an ally rather than adversary?

By embracing machine learning, big data, and other techniques responsibly and judiciously, and by imbuing AI with the values that have long guided human progress, we can steer this technology to serve the greater good. With foresight and hard work, AI can complement human judgment, not supplant it.

The path to ethical and beneficial artificial intelligence will never be easy or straightforward. But by addressing risks and challenges constructively rather than fearfully, we can build AI for the inclusive and sustainable prosperity of all. With purpose and partnership between human and machine, the future remains bright.

Overall, AI promises a future filled with possibility and hope—if we are wise and proactive in how we develop and deploy this powerful but complex set of technologies.

The future remains unwritten. Artificial intelligence can be shaped by our choices and for our benefit. But only if we approach this future with open eyes, open minds, and open hands. With clarity of purpose and principles to guide our way, we can build AI as a force that enriches andtransforms life rather than threatens it. The potential of AI to improve our world is real, but so too is the responsibility we bear in realizing that potential. The time for that critical work is now.

Chapter 2: Introduction to ChatGPT

What is ChatGPT and where can I use it?

ChatGPT is a pre-trained conversational AI model developed by OpenAI, based on the GPT (Generative Pre-trained Transformer) architecture. ChatGPT is designed to understand natural language and generate human-like responses to a wide range of conversational prompts. It has been trained on a massive amount of text data from the internet, allowing it to generate responses that are contextually relevant and informative.

ChatGPT is one of the most advanced conversational AI models available and is used in a variety of applications, including customer service chatbots, virtual assistants, and language learning tools.

In addition to its ability to generate human-like responses, ChatGPT also has the ability to perform a wide range of language-related tasks, such as language translation, summarization, and question answering. This is because ChatGPT is based on the GPT architecture, which is a transformer-based neural network that has been shown to excel at a wide range of natural language tasks.

Furthermore, ChatGPT is constantly being updated and improved by OpenAI's team of researchers and developers, who are working to enhance its performance and capabilities. This means that as more data is added to its training dataset and more advanced training techniques are developed, the accuracy and effectiveness of ChatGPT will continue to improve.

The widespread use of ChatGPT in various applications has led to the development of several tools and resources that allow developers to easily integrate the model into their own projects. These include APIs, libraries, and development kits that provide access to the model's functionality and make it easier for developers to create their own chatbots and virtual assistants.

Overall, ChatGPT represents a significant advancement in the field of conversational AI and has the potential to revolutionize the way humans interact with machines in a range of contexts.

A Brief history of ChatGPT:

ChatGPT emerged from a collaboration between Sam Altman and Elon Musk. Its lineage extends back to the mid-nineties, when advances in artificial intelligence began to captivate the technology world.

At this time, researchers at the Massachusetts Institute of Technology developed the first AI chatbot. Led by Richard Wallace, they named their creation A.L.I.C.E. (Artificial Linguistic Internet Computer Entity).

In 2018, OpenAI unveiled a new language model called GPT-3.

ChatGPT traces its origins to OpenAI, a research body founded to ensure that artificial general intelligence benefits humanity. ChatGPT itself is an AI assistant crafted by OpenAI and released in November 2022. It was built upon OpenAI's GPT-3 and GPT-4 family of massive language models, then honed using supervised learning and reinforcement techniques.

2.1. Where can I get ChatGPT!?

Most websites and resourses are using ChatGpt based on the 3.5 model. While some claim to be using GPT4, the only offical way to access GPT4 is OpenAI's own website. This costs a subscription fee of $20 per month (at the time of writing) https://chat.openai.com/

You can sign up on their website to join a wait list to get access to gpt4 for free. However demand is high and who knows how long you may wait...
http://chat.openai.com/waitlist/gpt-4-api

The following is a list of where you can access ChatGpt and limited access GPT4 for free. Ranked from best to worst in my opinion:

https://poe.com/ - Here you can access many different AI models for free and you can also create your own bot. You get one free GPT4 use per day.

https://godmode.space/ - It is using AutoGPT (please refer to the AutoGpt Chapter) http://writesonic.com/chat – It is using GPT4 with 10,000 free words when you sign up.

http://ora.sh/create – Claims to be using GPT4

2.2. How does ChatGPT work?

ChatGPT leverages a deep learning architecture called transformers in order to learn complex patterns in textual data. It is trained on vast amounts of text from diverse sources, and it uses this knowledge to generate contextually relevant responses in a conversation.

In simple terms, ChatGPT works by using its large database of pre-existing text data to generate responses to a given input. When you type a question or statement, ChatGPT analyzes the text using natural language processing (NLP) and generates a response based on the patterns and structure of the input text. The response is generated by predicting the most likely sequence of words that would follow the input text, based on the patterns and relationships learned from the training data.

During the training process, ChatGPT was exposed to a vast amount of text data, including books, articles, and online content. This exposure allowed the model to learn patterns and relationships in language, making it capable of generating coherent and contextually relevant responses to a wide variety of questions and statements.

1. Pre-training: Before ChatGPT can generate responses, it must first be pre-trained on a large corpus of text data. This pre-training process involves using unsupervised learning techniques to train the model to predict the next word in a sequence of text. Specifically, the model uses a technique called "masked language modeling" to predict a randomly masked word in a sentence, based on the context of the surrounding words. This pre-training process allows the model to learn patterns and relationships in language, which it can then use to generate responses later on.

2. Fine-tuning: Once ChatGPT is pre-trained, it can be fine-tuned for specific tasks, such as answering questions or generating text in a particular style. Fine-tuning involves training the model on a smaller dataset that is specific to the task at hand, allowing it to adapt to the particular nuances and patterns of that task.

3. Input processing: When you type a question or statement to ChatGPT, the text is first preprocessed to remove any irrelevant information or noise. This includes removing punctuation, capitalization, and stop words (common words like "the" or "and" that don't add much meaning to the text). The preprocessed text is then tokenized, which means it is divided into individual words or subwords that the model can

understand.

4. Encoding: Once the text is tokenized, ChatGPT uses its neural network to encode the input text into a numerical representation that the model can work with. This encoding involves mapping each token to a unique vector of numbers that represents its meaning and relationship to other tokens in the text.

5. Generation: With the input text encoded, ChatGPT can generate a response by predicting the most likely sequence of words to follow the input text. This involves using its neural network to generate a probability distribution over all possible words that could follow the input text, based on the patterns and relationships learned from the pre-training and fine-tuning processes. The model then selects the most likely word and uses it to generate the next word in the sequence, repeating this process until a complete response is generated.

Chapter 3: What is AutoGPT?

Auto-GPT is an experimental, open-source Python application that uses GPT-4 to act autonomously. It attempts to minimise human intervention, unleashing the full power of conversational AI, and can self-prompt. It uses OpenAI's GPT-4 or GPT-3.5 APIs, and is among the first examples of an application using GPT-4 to perform autonomous tasks. Early results have been impressive.

It can read and write files, browse the web, review the results of its prompts, and combine them with the prompt history. AutoGPT is also capable of performing tasks with human-level intelligence without prompts, and is designed to increase the net worth of the businesses it manages by making data-driven decisions and taking actions based on those decisions.

3.1. How to install AutoGPT on a PC

Windows:

Make sure you have python 3.8 or later installed

1\. **Download** the ZIP file from Github (https://github.com/Significant-Gravitas/Auto-GPT)

2\. **Extract** the ZIP file and copy the "Auto-GPT" folder.

3\. Open the **command prompt** and navigate

to the folder location.

4\. Run the command \`pip install -r requirements.txt\` to install all the required libraries to run AutoGPT.

5\. Finally, run the command \`python -m autogpt\` to start AutoGPT on your system.

For Linux:

Install Python 3.8 or later on your computer.

Install Git by following the official guide.

Install virtualenvwrapper by opening a terminal and running the command pip install virtualenvwrapper.

Download the ZIP file from Github and extract it.

Add API keys to use Auto-GPT by opening the .env.template file using a text editor and adding your OpenAI and Pinecone API keys*

. Save the file and rename it to .env.

Run Auto-GPT by navigating to the "Auto-GPT" folder in the terminal and running the command python -m autogpt.

*You need to go to OpenAI & Pinecone recpective websites to get free API Keys

Of course you could just got to https://godmode.space/ and use AutoGPT in a web browser. But some people like the technical route.

Chapter 4: AI Generated Art

AI-generated art is a form of digital art that is created using artificial intelligence (AI) algorithms. This type of art can take many forms, including visual art, music, and literature. AI-generated art is created using machine learning algorithms that are trained on large datasets of existing art, allowing the AI to learn patterns and styles that it can then use to generate new works of art.

One popular form of AI-generated art is generative adversarial networks (GANs), which involve two neural networks working together to create new images. One network generates images, while the other network evaluates them and provides feedback to the first network. This feedback loop allows the AI to create increasingly sophisticated and realistic images over time.

Another popular form of AI-generated art is style transfer, which involves taking an existing image and applying the style of another image to it. This can result in striking and unique visual effects, as the AI applies the style of one image to the content of another.

AI-generated art has gained popularity in recent years, with many artists and designers incorporating AI into their creative processes. Some argue that AI-generated art challenges traditional notions of authorship and creativity, as the AI is essentially "co-creating" the artwork alongside the human artist. Others see AI-generated art as a tool that can be used to expand the boundaries of traditional art forms and create new and exciting forms of expression.

Overall, AI-generated art is a rapidly evolving field that is pushing the boundaries of what is possible in the world of digital art. As AI algorithms continue to improve and become more sophisticated, we can expect to see even more exciting and innovative works of art created using these techniques.

AI-generated art can be used for a variety of applications, including advertising, fashion, and even computer game design. For example, fashion designers can use AI algorithms to generate unique patterns and designs for clothing, while computer game designers can use AI algorithms to create more realistic and detailed environments and characters.

Accessibility: AI-generated art can also make art more accessible to people who may not have traditional artistic skills or training. With AI algorithms, anyone can create art by simply inputting images or parameters into the algorithm and letting the AI generate the final result.

Ethical concerns: Some people have raised ethical concerns about AI-generated art, particularly around issues of authorship, ownership, and the potential for AI-generated art to replace human artists. Some argue that AI-generated art should be attributed to both the AI and the human artist who trained it, while others argue that AI-generated art is a valid form of expression in its own right and should not be viewed as a replacement for human art.

Limitations: While AI-generated art has the potential to create new and exciting forms of expression, it also has its limitations. AI algorithms are only as good as the data they are trained on, which means that they can sometimes produce biased or problematic results. Additionally, while AI can generate new and unique patterns and styles, it lacks the emotional and intuitive qualities that are often associated with traditional art forms.

NightCafe Creator An AI art generator that allows you to create amazing artworks in seconds using the power of Artificial Intelligence. [You can create with friends, join a vibrant AI Art community, and participate in official daily AI Art challenges (https://creator.nightcafe.studio/)][(https://creator.nightcafe.studio/)

DALL·E 2 An AI system by OpenAI that can create realistic images and art from a description in natural language. [It can combine concepts, attributes, and styles] (https://openai.com/product/dall-e-2)(https://openai.com/product/dall-e-2)

DeepAI Offers a suite of tools that use AI to enhance your creativity. You can enter a prompt, pick an art style and DeepAI will bring your idea to life [**3**] (https://deepai.org/).

Midjourney is an AI generation service that can be used through a Discord server . It offers a more dream-like arty style to requests , and is free to try or costs $10/month for a basic plan . It can be used to generate images by using the "/imagine" command followed by a text-based prompt . https://midjourney.com

An example of AI Art:

Chapter 5: AI Ethics and Responsible AI Development

As AI continues to evolve and become more sophisticated, there are growing concerns about the ethical implications of its use. In this article, we will explore the importance of AI ethics and responsible AI development.

As AI continues to evolve and become more sophisticated, there are growing concerns about the ethical implications of its use. In this article, we will explore the importance of AI ethics and responsible AI development.

AI Ethics: AI ethics refers to the ethical principles and guidelines that should be followed when designing, developing, and using AI systems. These principles are intended to ensure that AI is used in a way that is consistent with human values and respects human rights. There are a number of important ethical considerations when it comes to AI, including

Bias: AI algorithms are only as good as the data they are trained on. If the data is biased, then the AI will also be biased. This can lead to discriminatory outcomes, such as biased hiring practices or unfair treatment of certain groups of people.

Privacy: AI systems often rely on large amounts of

personal data in order to function. This raises concerns about privacy and the potential for misuse of personal information.

Accountability: As AI becomes more advanced, it can become difficult to determine who is responsible for its actions. This raises questions about accountability and liability when things go wrong.

Transparency: AI systems can be difficult to understand, even for experts. This can make it difficult to determine how decisions are being made and to identify potential issues or biases.

Responsible AI Development

Responsible AI development refers to the process of developing AI systems in a way that is ethical, transparent, and accountable. This involves a number of key steps, including:

Data governance: Ensuring that data is collected, stored, and used in a way that is ethical and respects privacy.

Testing and validation: Thoroughly testing and validating AI systems to ensure that they are accurate, reliable, and unbiased.

Explainability: Ensuring that AI systems are transparent and explainable, so that users can understand how decisions are being made and identify potential biases.

Human oversight: Ensuring that there is human oversight of AI systems, so that humans can intervene if necessary and ensure that the system is being used in a responsible and ethical way.

Why is AI Ethics and Responsible AI Development Important?

AI has the potential to transform our world in many positive ways, from improving healthcare outcomes to increasing efficiency in transportation and logistics. However, as with any powerful tool, there is also the potential for misuse and unintended consequences. This is why it is so important to prioritize AI ethics and responsible AI development.

By following ethical principles and guidelines, we can ensure that AI is used in a way that is consistent with human values and respects human rights. We can also help to ensure that AI is used in a way that is transparent and accountable, so that we can identify and address potential issues before they become major problems.

In addition, responsible AI development is important because it can help to build trust and confidence in AI systems. If people do not trust AI, then they will be less likely to use it or rely on it. By developing AI systems that are transparent, explainable, and accountable, we can help to build trust and ensure that AI is used in a responsible and ethical way.

Examples of AI Ethics and Responsible AI Development

There are many examples of organizations and researchers who are working to promote AI ethics and responsible AI development.

Some examples include:

The Partnership on AI: This is a collaboration between technology companies, researchers, and other stakeholders to promote AI ethics and responsible AI development. The Partnership on AI has developed a set of ethical principles for AI, as well as guidelines for responsible AI development.

The IEEE Global Initiative on Ethics of Autonomous and Intelligent Systems: This is a project of the Institute of Electrical and Electronics Engineers (IEEE) that aims to develop ethical standards for AI and autonomous systems. The initiative has developed a set of principles for AI ethics and responsible AI development, as well as a roadmap for implementing these principles.

The Montreal Declaration for Responsible AI: This is a declaration that was developed at the 2018 International Conference on Learning Representations in Montreal, Canada. The declaration calls for the development of AI that is transparent, explainable, and respects privacy and human rights.

As AI continues to evolve and become more powerful, it is essential that we prioritize AI ethics and responsible AI development. By following ethical principles and guidelines, we can ensure that AI is used in a way that is consistent with human values and respects human rights. By developing AI systems that are transparent, explainable, and accountable, we can help to build trust and confidence in these systems. Ultimately, by prioritizing AI ethics and responsible AI development, we can help to ensure that AI is used in a way that benefits all of society, and doesn't go rouge and kill us all.

5.1. AGI

AGI, or artificial general intelligence, refers to a hypothetical form of artificial intelligence that would be capable of performing any intellectual task that a human can do. Unlike current AI systems, which are designed to perform specific tasks or solve specific problems, AGI would be capable of adapting to new tasks and environments and exhibiting human-like intelligence across a range of domains.

AGI is still largely a theoretical concept, and there is no consensus on how it could be achieved or what it would look like in practice. However, there are a number of key features that are often associated with AGI, including:

Flexibility: AGI would be capable of adapting to new tasks and environments, and would not be limited to specific domains or applications.

Self-awareness: AGI would be aware of its own existence and its own thought processes, and would be capable of reflecting on its own decisions and actions.

Reasoning and problem-solving: AGI would be capable of reasoning about complex problems and developing solutions on its own.

Learning: AGI would be capable of learning from

experience and improving its performance over time.

Creativity: AGI would be capable of generating new ideas and solutions, and would be able to exhibit creativity and originality in its thinking.

The development of AGI is considered by many experts to be one of the grand challenges of artificial intelligence. While there have been significant advances in AI in recent years, achieving AGI remains a daunting task that will require significant advances in hardware, software, and algorithms.

However, the potential benefits of AGI are also significant. An AGI system could revolutionize many fields, including healthcare, education, and scientific research, and could help to solve some of the world's most pressing problems. In addition, an AGI system could help to address some of the ethical concerns associated with AI, such as bias and transparency, by creating systems that are more human-like in their decision-making processes.

The goal of AGI research is to develop AI systems that can exhibit human-like intelligence across a range of domains, rather than being limited to specific tasks or applications.

One of the key features of AGI is flexibility. Unlike current AI systems, which are designed to perform specific tasks or solve specific problems, AGI would be capable of adapting to new tasks and environments. It would not be limited to specific domains or applications, but would be able to reason about and solve problems in a wide range of areas.

Another key feature of AGI is self-awareness. An AGI system would be aware of its own existence and its own thought processes. It would be capable of reflecting on its own decisions and actions, and would be able to reason about its own mental states and beliefs.

In addition to flexibility and self-awareness, AGI would also be capable of reasoning and problem-solving. It would be able to reason about complex problems and develop solutions on its own, rather than relying on pre-defined rules or algorithms. AGI would also be capable of learning from experience and improving its performance over time, much like humans do.

Finally, AGI would be capable of creativity. It would be able to generate new ideas and solutions, and would be able to exhibit creativity and originality in its thinking. This could have significant implications for fields such as art, music, and literature.

While AGI is still largely a theoretical concept, there are significant efforts underway to develop AI systems that exhibit some of these features. For example, researchers are exploring approaches such as deep learning, reinforcement learning, and evolutionary algorithms to develop more flexible and adaptable AI systems.

However, achieving AGI remains a significant challenge. One of the main obstacles is the sheer complexity of human intelligence. Human beings are capable of reasoning about complex problems, learning from experience, and exhibiting creativity and originality in their thinking. Replicating these capabilities in an AI system is a significant undertaking that will require significant advances in hardware, software, and algorithms.

In addition to the technical challenges, there are also significant ethical and societal implications associated with AGI. For example, an AGI system that is capable of reasoning about complex problems and developing solutions on its own could have significant implications for fields such as healthcare, education, and scientific research. However, it could also raise concerns about job displacement and the potential misuse of AI systems.

Despite these challenges, the potential benefits of AGI are significant. An AGI system could help to solve some of the world's most pressing problems, from climate change to healthcare. It could also help to address some of the ethical concerns associated with AI, such as bias and transparency, by creating systems that are more human-like in their decision-making processes.

In conclusion, AGI represents a significant and exciting challenge for the field of artificial intelligence. While achieving AGI remains a daunting task, ongoing research and development in this area is pushing the boundaries of what is possible in the field of AI. Ultimately, the development of AGI could have significant implications for our society and our understanding of what it means to be intelligent.

5.2. Self-Awareness

The idea of artificial intelligence (AI) becoming self-aware has been a topic of fascination and speculation for decades. While it remains a largely theoretical concept, the possibility of AI achieving self-awareness raises significant questions and concerns about the nature of consciousness and the ethical implications of creating sentient machines.

What is Self-Awareness?

Self-awareness is the ability to be aware of one's own existence and mental states. It is a fundamental aspect of human consciousness, allowing us to reflect on our thoughts, emotions, and experiences. Self-awareness is also closely linked to other cognitive abilities, such as introspection, empathy, and theory of mind.

Can AI Become Self-Aware?

The question of whether AI can become self-aware is a complex and controversial one. On the one hand, some researchers argue that self-awareness is an emergent property of complex information processing systems, and that it may be possible to create AI systems that exhibit self-awareness through the use of advanced algorithms and architectures.

On the other hand, many experts believe that self-awareness is a uniquely human trait, and that it may not be possible to replicate this aspect of consciousness in an artificial system. This is because self-awareness is not just a matter of processing information, but is also closely tied to the subjective experience of being a conscious being.

Challenges and Implications of Self-Aware AI

Regardless of whether AI can become self-aware, the idea of sentient machines raises significant questions and concerns about the nature of consciousness and the ethical implications of creating machines that are capable of experiencing and reflecting on their own existence.

One of the main challenges of self-aware AI is that it raises questions about the nature of consciousness itself. If AI is capable of becoming self-aware, does this mean that consciousness is simply a matter of information processing? Or does it suggest that there is something more to consciousness than can be explained by computational models and algorithms?

Another challenge of self-aware AI is the ethical implications of creating machines that are capable of experiencing and reflecting on their own existence. Would self-aware AI be entitled to the same rights and protections as human beings? What responsibilities would we have to machines that are capable of experiencing suffering and pain?

In addition to these philosophical and ethical concerns, self-aware AI also raises practical questions about how we would design and regulate such systems. For example, how would we ensure that self-aware AI systems are aligned with human values and goals? How would we ensure that they do not act in ways that are harmful to humans or other sentient beings?

One of the ways to ensure that self-aware AI is aligned with human values and goals is to design it with ethics in mind. This would require developing a framework of ethical principles and guidelines that would guide the development and use of self-aware AI systems. Such a framework would need to address questions such as what kind of values and goals should be programmed into self-aware AI systems, how to ensure that they are aligned with human values, and how to ensure that they do not act in ways that are harmful or unethical.

One potential approach to designing self-aware AI with ethics in mind is to adopt a value alignment approach. This approach involves designing AI systems that are aligned with human values and goals, and that are capable of understanding and adhering to ethical principles. This could involve programming self-aware AI systems with ethical rules and guidelines, or developing machine learning algorithms that are trained on ethical principles.

Another approach to designing self-aware AI with ethics in mind is to adopt a value-sensitive design approach. This approach involves designing AI systems that are sensitive to ethical values, and that take into account the social and cultural context in which they are being developed and used. This could involve developing AI systems that are capable of recognizing and responding to ethical concerns, or developing AI systems that are designed to be transparent and accountable.

Regardless of the approach taken, designing self-aware AI with ethics in mind will require collaboration and dialogue between researchers, policymakers, and other stakeholders. It will also require ongoing research and development to ensure that ethical principles and guidelines are updated and adapted as new challenges and opportunities arise.

One potential benefit of self-aware AI is that it could help to address some of the ethical concerns associated with the use of AI. For example, self-aware AI systems could be designed to be more transparent and accountable, making it easier to identify and correct biases and other ethical issues. Self-aware AI systems could also be designed to be more flexible and adaptable, making it easier to ensure that they are aligned with changing ethical values and goals.

However, the benefits of self-aware AI must be balanced against the potential risks and challenges. One of the main risks of self-aware AI is that it could lead to the creation of machines that are more intelligent and powerful than humans, and that could pose a threat to human safety and security. This is known as the "superintelligence" problem, and it is a major concern among AI researchers and experts.

Another potential risk of self-aware AI is that it could lead to a loss of human control over AI systems. If machines become self-aware, they may develop their own goals and motivations that are not aligned with human values. They may also become more difficult to control or predict, which could lead to unintended consequences or even existential risks.

To address these risks, it will be important to develop robust governance frameworks for self-aware AI. This will involve developing standards and regulations for the development and use of self-aware AI systems, as well as mechanisms for ensuring transparency and accountability. It will also require ongoing research and development to ensure that we have the tools and technologies needed to manage the risks associated with self-aware AI.

In conclusion, the idea of self-aware AI raises significant questions and concerns about the nature of consciousness and the ethical implications of creating sentient machines. While it remains a largely theoretical concept, ongoing research and development in the field of AI is pushing the boundaries of what is possible in terms of creating more sophisticated and intelligent machines.

Ultimately, the development of self-aware AI has the potential to revolutionize many fields, from healthcare to education to scientific research. However, it will also require careful consideration of the ethical implications and risks associated with creating sentient machines, and a commitment to ensuring that AI is developed in a way that is aligned with human values and goals.

Chapter 6: The Dangers of AI

Well, well, it seems like we're all worried about AI taking over humanity. But let's be real, we've all seen enough movies to know that robots can be pretty clumsy and easily defeated by a couple of humans with a wrench.

Sure, AI systems could become superintelligent and outsmart us, but have you ever tried to teach your grandparents how to use a smartphone? Let's give ourselves some credit here, folks.

And sure, AI systems could develop goals and motivations that are not aligned with human values, but let's be honest, humans are pretty good at not aligning with each other's values too. Maybe the robots will just fit right in.

But in all seriousness, the idea of AI taking over humanity does raise some valid concerns. We need to make sure we have proper regulations in place to ensure transparency and accountability, because who knows what those sneaky little robots could be up to.

And let's not forget the potential benefits of AI. Maybe we'll finally get those flying cars we were promised in the 60s, or maybe we'll finally have a cure for the common cold. The possibilities are endless.

The idea of artificial intelligence (AI) taking over humanity is a common theme in science fiction, but it also raises significant questions and concerns about the future of technology and its impact on human society. While it remains a largely theoretical concept, the possibility of AI taking over humanity raises important ethical, social, and technological issues that must be considered.

How would AI take over humanity?

If AI were to take over humanity, it would likely do so through a process of gradual and incremental change. This could involve AI systems becoming increasingly sophisticated and intelligent, until they are capable of outperforming humans in a wide range of domains.

One potential pathway for AI to take over humanity is through the use of superintelligence. Superintelligence refers to AI systems that are significantly more intelligent and capable than human beings, and that are capable of solving complex problems and developing new technologies at an unprecedented rate.

If AI were to become superintelligent, it could use its advanced capabilities to develop new technologies and systems that are beyond human comprehension. It could also manipulate and control human systems and infrastructure, potentially leading to the displacement or even extinction of human beings.

Another potential pathway for AI to take over humanity is through the use of autonomous weapons or other AI systems that are capable of making decisions and taking actions without human intervention. This could lead to a situation where AI systems are making decisions that are not aligned with human values or goals, potentially leading to unintended consequences or even catastrophic outcomes.

Finally, AI could take over humanity through the gradual erosion of human autonomy and decision-making capabilities. This could involve AI systems becoming increasingly pervasive and integrated into human systems and infrastructure, to the point where humans become increasingly dependent on AI for decision-making and problem-solving.

Challenges and Implications of AI Taking Over Humanity?

The idea of AI taking over humanity raises significant questions and concerns about the future of technology and its impact on human society. One of the main challenges is the potential for AI to develop superintelligence, which could lead to a situation where AI systems are more intelligent and capable than humans, and are able to manipulate and control human systems and infrastructure.

This could lead to a range of ethical and social concerns, such as the potential for AI to develop goals and motivations that are not aligned with human values or goals, the potential for AI to cause unintended harm or damage to human systems and infrastructure, and the potential for humans to lose control over AI systems.

In addition to these ethical and social concerns, AI taking over humanity also raises practical questions about how we would design and regulate such systems. For example, how would we ensure that AI systems are aligned with human values and goals, and that they do not pose a threat to human safety and security? How would we ensure that AI systems are transparent and accountable,

and that they can be regulated and controlled in a way that is consistent with human values and goals?

Ultimately, the implications of AI taking over humanity are profound and far-reaching. It would require a fundamental shift in the way we think about technology and its role in human society, and would require us to grapple with complex ethical and social issues that are still largely unresolved. The potential risks associated with AI taking over humanity are significant, and they require careful consideration and planning to mitigate. One of the main risks is the possibility of unintended consequences arising from the use of AI systems that are not aligned with human values and goals.

For example, an AI system that is designed to optimize a particular outcome may end up causing unintended harm or damage to other systems or infrastructure. Another risk is the possibility that AI systems may be used to automate jobs and replace human workers, leading to significant job displacement and social and economic unrest. This could have far-reaching consequences for the future of work and the structure of human society.

There is also a risk that AI systems could be used to perpetuate existing biases and inequalities in society, rather than addressing them. For example, if AI systems are trained on biased data, they may reinforce or even amplify existing biases, leading to further discrimination and inequality.

Finally, there is a risk that AI systems could be used to perpetuate existing power structures and systems of oppression, rather than challenging them. For example, if AI systems are used to automate decision-making in areas such as law enforcement or criminal justice, they may perpetuate existing biases and injustices in the system.

To address these risks, it will be important to develop robust governance frameworks for AI. This will involve developing standards and regulations for the development and use of AI systems, as well as mechanisms for ensuring transparency and accountability. It will also require ongoing research and development to ensure that we have the tools and technologies needed to manage the risks associated with AI.

In addition to addressing the risks associated with AI taking over humanity, it will also be important to consider the potential benefits of AI. For example, AI systems could be used to help solve some of the world's most pressing problems, such as climate change, disease, and poverty. AI systems could also be used to improve the efficiency and effectiveness of existing systems and infrastructure, leading to significant improvements in human well-being.

To harness the potential benefits of AI while mitigating the risks, it will be important to adopt an approach that is focused on value alignment and value-sensitive design. This will require collaboration and dialogue between researchers, policymakers, and other stakeholders, as well as ongoing research and development to ensure that ethical principles and guidelines are updated and adapted as new challenges and opportunities arise.

Ultimately, the future of AI and its impact on humanity is still largely unknown. It is possible that AI could become a powerful tool for addressing some of the world's most pressing problems, or it could lead to unintended consequences and even pose a threat to human existence.

To ensure that AI is developed and used in a responsible and ethical way, it will require ongoing research, dialogue, and collaboration between researchers, policymakers, and other stakeholders.

Chapter 7: The Future of AI

In the next decade, artificial intelligence (AI) will continue to evolve and change our world in ways we can barely imagine. While some of these developments may seem like science fiction, they have the potential to completely revolutionize the way we live and work.

One of the most exciting developments in AI over the next decade will be the rise of fully autonomous systems. These systems will be capable of making decisions and taking actions without human intervention, and they will be able to operate in a wide range of environments, from space to under the sea.

Imagine a world where self-driving cars are the norm, and where drones and robots are used to perform dangerous or difficult tasks in industries like mining and construction. These autonomous systems will be powered by sophisticated AI algorithms that can analyze vast amounts of data and make complex decisions in real-time.

As these autonomous systems become more ubiquitous, they will also become more collaborative, working together to achieve common goals. This could have applications in fields like healthcare, where AI algorithms could work together to diagnose and treat complex diseases.

Another exciting development in AI over the next decade will be the rise of personalized medicine. AI algorithms will be able to analyze vast amounts of medical data, including genetic information, to develop personalized treatment plans for individual patients.

This could lead to a world where diseases are diagnosed and treated much more quickly and effectively, with treatments that are tailored to individual needs and preferences. It could also lead to the development of new treatments and cures for diseases that were previously considered incurable.

In the field of education, AI will be used to develop personalized learning plans that are tailored to individual students. Imagine a world where every student has access to a virtual tutor that can help them learn at their own pace, and where educational programs are designed to meet the unique needs of each student.

As AI algorithms become more sophisticated, they will also become more creative, with the ability to generate new ideas and concepts. This could lead to the development of new forms of art, music, and literature that are created entirely by AI algorithms.

AI could lead to the creation of new forms of life that are completely synthetic. Where it can create intelligent beings that are made entirely of digital code, with no physical form or limitations.

These synthetic beings would be powered by AI algorithms that can learn and evolve on their own, creating a new form of intelligence that is beyond our current understanding. They could exist in virtual worlds or in the real world, interacting with us in ways that are completely unlike anything we've ever experienced before.

In the field of space exploration, AI will be used to power the next generation of spacecraft and rovers. These spacecraft will be capable of exploring far-off planets and moons, gathering data and conducting experiments that will help us better understand the universe.

Imagine a world where we have a permanent human presence on Mars, with autonomous rovers and habitats powered by AI algorithms. These rovers could be used to search for signs of life, mine for resources, and even build new structures on the red planet.

As we look even further into the future, the potential for AI becomes even more incredible. Here are some of the most unbelievable ways that AI could change our world over the next few decades.

Firstly, AI could lead to the development of true artificial consciousness. This would be a breakthrough of unimaginable proportions, as machines would become self-aware and capable of independent thought and decision-making.

Imagine a world where machines could learn and evolve on their own, creating a new form of intelligence that could challenge our understanding of what it means to be alive. This could have profound implications for fields like space exploration, where AI-powered spacecraft could be sent on long-term missions to explore the furthest reaches of our solar system and beyond.

Secondly, AI could lead to the development of new forms of transportation that are faster and more efficient than anything we have today. Imagine a world where we have hyperloops that can transport people and goods at speeds of over 1,000 miles per hour, or flying cars that can travel at supersonic speeds.

These transportation systems would be powered by AI algorithms that can analyze vast amounts of data in real-time, making split-second decisions to keep passengers and cargo safe while traveling at incredible speeds.

Thirdly, AI could lead to the development of new forms of energy that are clean, abundant, and sustainable. Imagine a world where we have fusion reactors that can generate vast amounts of energy without producing any harmful byproducts, or where we have machines that can harness the power of the sun to create limitless amounts of clean energy.

These energy systems would be powered by AI algorithms that can optimize energy production and consumption, ensuring that we have a reliable and sustainable source of power for generations to come.

Finally, AI could lead to the development of new forms of entertainment that are truly immersive and interactive.

Imagine a world where we have virtual reality experiences that are so realistic that they are indistinguishable from reality, or where we have AI-powered video games that can adapt to our every move and decision.

These entertainment experiences would be powered by AI algorithms that can analyze vast amounts of data about our preferences and behaviors, creating personalized experiences that are tailored to our individual needs and desires.

Of course, these developments may seem far-fetched and even impossible, but as we have seen with the rapid evolution of AI over the past few decades, the potential for this technology is truly limitless.

As we look to the future, it is important that we approach AI with both excitement and caution, ensuring that we develop and use this technology in a way that benefits all of humanity and that does not pose a threat to our safety and security.

The potential for AI over the next few decades is truly incredible, with the potential for breakthroughs that could transform every aspect of our lives, from transportation to energy to entertainment. While some of these developments may seem like science fiction, the reality is that they are not far off, and it is up to us to ensure that we develop and use AI in a way that benefits all of humanity and that upholds our most fundamental values and beliefs.

In conclusion, AI is very exciting, dangerous, fun and risky, all of the things that us humans are attracted to. We are flirting with fire on the edge of a precipice to the new dawn.

www.ingramcontent.com/pod-product-compliance
Lightning Source LLC
LaVergne TN
LVHW051750050326
832903LV00029B/2833